KUMITE 1

BEST KARATE 3

Kumite 1

M. Nakayama

KODANSHA INTERNATIONAL LTD.

Tokyo, New York & San Francisco

Front cover photo by Keizō Kaneko; demonstration photos by Yoshinao Murai.

Distributed in the United States by Kodansha International/USA Ltd., through Harper & Row, Publishers, Inc., 10 East 53rd Street, New York, New York 10022.

Published by Kodansha International Ltd., 12-21, Otowa 2-chome, Bunkyo-ku, Tokyo 112 and Kodansha International/USA Ltd., with offices at 10 East 53rd Street, New York, New York 10022 and The Hearst Building, 5 Third Street, Suite No. 430, San Francisco, California 94103. Copyright © 1978 by Kodansha International Ltd. All rights reserved. Printed in Japan.
LCC 77-74829
ISBN 0-87011-332-1
ISBN 4-7700-0648-9 (in Japan)

First edition, 1978
Fifth printing, 1984

CONTENTS

Dedicated
to my teacher
GICHIN FUNAKOSHI
and to
MINORU MIYATA

INTRODUCTION

The past decade has seen a great increase in the popularity of karate-dō throughout the world. Among those who have been attracted to it are college students and teachers, artists, businessmen and civil servants. It has come to be practiced by policemen and members of Japan's Self-defense Forces. In a number of universities, it has become a compulsory subject, and that number is increasing yearly.

Along with the increase in popularity, there have been certain unfortunate and regrettable interpretations and performances. For one thing, karate has been confused with the so-called Chinese-style boxing, and its relationship with the original Okinawan *Te* has not been sufficiently understood. There are also people who have regarded it as a mere show, in which two men attack each other savagely, or the contestants battle each other as though it were a form of boxing in which the feet are used, or a man shows off by breaking bricks or other hard objects with his head, hand or foot.

If karate is practiced solely as a fighting technique, this is cause for regret. The fundamental techniques have been developed and perfected through long years of study and practice, but to make any effective use of these techniques, the spiritual aspect of this art of self-defense must be recognized and must play the predominant role. It is gratifying to me to see that there are those who understand this, who know that karate-dō is a purely Oriental martial art, and who train with the proper attitude.

To be capable of inflicting devastating damage on an opponent with one blow of the fist or a single kick has indeed been the objective of this ancient Okinawan martial art. But even the practitioners of old placed stronger emphasis on the spiritual side of the art than on the techniques. Training means training of body and spirit, and, above all else, one should treat his opponent courteously and with the proper etiquette. It is not enough to fight with all one's power; the real objective in karate-dō is to do so for the sake of justice.

Gichin Funakoshi, a great master of karate-dō, pointed out repeatedly that the first purpose in pursuing this art is the nurturing of a sublime spirit, a spirit of humility. Simultaneously, power sufficient to destroy a ferocious wild animal with a single blow should be developed. Becoming a true follower of karate-dō is possible only when one attains perfection in these two aspects, the one spiritual, the other physical.

Karate as an art of self-defense and karate as a means of improving and maintaining health has long existed. During the past twenty years, a new activity has been explored and is coming to the fore. This is *sports karate.*

In sports karate, contests are held for the purpose of determining the ability of the participants. This needs emphasizing, for here again there is cause for regret. There is a tendency to place too much emphasis on winning contests, and those who do so neglect the practice of fundamental techniques, opting instead to attempt jiyū kumite at the earliest opportunity.

Emphasis on winning contests cannot help but alter the fundamental techniques a person uses and the practice he engages in. Not only that, it will result in a person's being incapable of executing a strong and effective technique, which, after all, is the unique characteristic of karate-dō. The man who begins jiyū kumite prematurely—without having practiced fundamentals sufficiently—will soon be overtaken by the man who has trained in the basic techniques long and diligently. It is, quite simply, a matter of haste makes waste. There is no alternative to learning and practicing basic techniques and movements step by step, stage by stage.

If karate competitions are to be held, they must be conducted under suitable conditions and in the proper spirit. The desire to win a contest is counterproductive, since it leads to a lack of seriousness in learning the fundamentals. Moreover, aiming for a savage display of strength and power in a contest is totally undesirable. When this happens, courtesy toward the opponent is forgotten, and this is of prime importance in any expression of karate. I believe this matter deserves a great deal of reflection and self-examination by both instructors and students.

To explain the many and complex movements of the body, it has been my desire to present a fully illustrated book with an up-to-date text, based on the experience in this art that I have acquired over a period of forty-six years. This hope is being realized by the publication of the *Best Karate* series, in which earlier writings of mine have been totally revised with the help and encouragement of my readers. This new series explains in detail what karate-dō is in language made as simple as possible, and I sincerely hope that it will be of help to followers of karate-dō. I hope also that karateka in many countries will be able to understand each other better through this series of books.

Deciding who is the winner and who is the loser is not the ultimate objective. Karate-dō is a martial art for the development of character through training, so that the karateka can surmount any obstacle, tangible or intangible.

Karate-dō is an empty-handed art of self-defense in which the arms and legs are systematically trained and an enemy attacking by surprise can be controlled by a demonstration of strength like that of using actual weapons.

Karate-dō is exercise through which the karateka masters all body movements, such as bending, jumping and balancing, by learning to move limbs and body backward and forward, left and right, up and down, freely and uniformly.

The techniques of karate-dō are well controlled according to the karateka's will power and are directed at the target accurately and spontaneously.

The essence of karate techniques is *kime.* The meaning of *kime* is an explosive attack to the target using the appropriate technique and maximum power in the shortest time possible. (Long ago, there was the expression *ikken hissatsu,* meaning "to kill with one blow," but to assume from this that killing is the objective is dangerous and incorrect. It should be remembered that the karateka of old were able to practice *kime* daily and in dead seriousness by using the makiwara.)

Kime may be accomplished by striking, punching or kicking, but also by blocking. A technique lacking *kime* can never be regarded as true karate, no matter how great the resemblance to karate. A contest is no exception; however, it is against the rules to make contact because of the danger involved.

Sun-dome means to arrest a technique just before contact with the target (one *sun,* about three centimeters). But not carrying a technique through to *kime* is not true karate, so the question is how to reconcile the contradiction between *kime* and *sun-dome.* The answer is this: establish the target slightly in front of the opponent's vital point. It can then be hit in a controlled way with maximum power, without making contact.

Training transforms various parts of the body into weapons to be used freely and effectively. The quality necessary to accomplish this is self-control. To become a victor, one must first overcome his own self.

Organization of volumes 3 and 4

Volumes 3 and 4 of the Best Karate series give a selection of techniques, tactics and strategy applicable in kumite training. These are organized, chapter by chapter, so as to give guidance to the beginner for improvement. I have used a large number of photographs but rather few words. I hope you will study both with care and train with diligence.

Techniques used in kumite are demonstrated by instructors of the Japan Karate Association as follows:

This volume:

Sen no Sen	Takeshi Ōishi, Shunsuke Takahashi
Go no Sen	Norihiko Iida, Yoshiharu Ōsaka
Types of Kicks	Masaaki Ueki, Mikio Yahara
Striking in Close Combat	Keigo Abe, Mikio Yahara
Kicking in Close Combat	Katsunori Tsuyama, Eishige Matsukura
Rotation, Tai-sabaki, Throwing	Tetsuhiko Asai, Yoshiharu Ōsaka
Two-level Attack	Hirokazu Kanazawa, Yoshiharu Ōsaka

Volume 4:

Kuzushi, Leg Sweep	Keinosuke Enoeda, Fujikiyo Ōmura
Changing Techniques	Toru Yamaguchi, Yoshiki Satō
Cutting Kick	Masahiko Tanaka, Masao Kawazoe
Response to Punch or Kick	Masao Kawazoe, Yoshiharu Ōsaka
Last-chance Technique	Mikio Yahara, Takashi Naito
Continuous Techniques	Hiroshi Shōji, Toru Yamaguchi
Blocking Kime	Masatoshi Nakayama, Yoshiharu Ōsaka

To help the karateka to understand the spirit and mental attitude of the martial arts, there are selections from:

Fudō chishin myōroku by Takuan Zenji
Heihoka densho by Yagyū Munenori
Gorin no sho by Miyamoto Musashi
Ittōsai sensei kenpō sho by Kotōda Yahei

1
KUMITE

MEANING AND TYPES

The Meaning of Kumite

Kumite is a method of training in which the offensive and defensive techniques learned in the kata are given pratical application. The opponents are face to face.

The importance of kata to kumite cannot be overemphasized. If techniques are used unnaturally or in a forced way, posture will break down. And if the kata techniques become confused when applied, no improvement in kumite can be expected. In other words, improvement in kumite depends directly on improvement in kata; the two go together like hand in glove. It is a mistake to emphasize one at the expense of the other. This is a point to be careful about when practicing kumite.

The Types of Kumite

Basic kumite, jiyū ippon kumite and jiyū kumite are the three types of kumite.

Basic kumite

In this most elementary form of kumite, the opponents take a fixed distance from each other and the target area is agreed on beforehand. They then alternately practice attacking and blocking. This may be done as a single attack and block—*ippon kumite*—or a series of five—*gohon kumite* (also three, *sambon kumite*). (See Vol. 1, pp. 112—20.)

Jiyū ippon kumite and jiyū kumite

The late Minoru Miyata was my classmate and a colleague of mine since the founding of the Japan Karate Association. From his long years of experience, he held a clearly defined view of jiyū ippon kumite and jiyū kumite. Since he was a man whose capabilities were highly evaluated by others and one in whom I had very great confidence, I would like to quote him on this subject.

The method of ippon jiyū kumite is this. Both men take a *kamae* freely at an optional distance. [*Kamae,* posture, specifically that of the torso and arms.] Announcing the area he is aiming for, the attacker attacks decisively. Against this the blocker freely uses techniques he has mastered and counterattacks at once. This is a training method; the purpose is to put into actual practice the techniques of offense and defense. This is *jissen* (actual fighting) kumite.

In this way, the attacker, gauging *maai* and *kokyū* (breathing) and making use of feints and so on, takes advantage of any opening and with good timing develops his attacking strength. The blocker, advancing, retreating or executing *tai-sabaki* to left or right, uses his techniques in any direction and counterattacks. Because it involves methods of attack and defense in all directions, *kokyū*, *maai*, *tai-sabaki*, shifting the center of gravity, blocking-finishing in one breath, jiyū ippon kumite is an extremely important method for forging techniques.

There is this way of thinking about jiyū ippon kumite. If after attacking, the attacker deceives the blocker and continues to attack, or if he attacks without announcing his intention by turning the blocker's counterattack against him, this training method will become jiyū kumite. This preliminary step to jiyū kumite requires great skill, so it cannot be recommended to beginners, whose techniques will break down and become ineffective. Only for the skilled is this a good method of cultivating true sight, the sixth sense of attack and defense. [See Vol 2, p. 101.]

The tendency recently is to advance to jiyū kumite prematurely, and the result of this—*kime* lacking intense, strong power—is seen far too often, because the participants in contests lack sufficient training in fundamentals and kata. This approach is defective, but I believe it is on the increase. To correct this, instead of taking jiyū ippon kumite as the preliminary step to jiyū kumite, it is of the utmost necessity in the first place to master strong techniques one by one through correct training and, at the same, *maai*, *kokyū*, *tai-sabaki*, and so on. Then ippon kumite can be the gateway to jiyū kumite.

Judō has its *randori*, karate-dō its jiyū kumite, to be engaged in without prearrangement. A number of techniques and targets are prohibited. With due regard for this point, it is a free form of *jissen*.

From ancient days when techniques were secret and practiced individually, kata were at the core of training and reached an extremely high level of meaning. Today's karate-dō is also training through kata. As for kumite, basic prearranged kumite was a form of training from a fairly long time ago, but it was only when karate began to thrive in universities and other places in the late 1920s that jiyū kumite was introduced. Training through gohon kumite gained momentum, and this lead to *shizen* (natural) and *jiyū* (free) kumite. Jiyū kumite appeared officially for the first time on a public program in 1936, when a tournament was held commemorating the establishment of the Japan Student Karate-dō Federation. Compared with judō and kendō, this was a late start, and with the inevitable development of sports karate, much deeper research in jiyū kumite must be done.

Essential to training through jiyū kumite are *kamaekata, tachikata, me no tsukekata, maai* and *waza o hodokosu kōki.*

1. *Kamaekata,* posture, specifically of the upper body

Kamaekata must be such as to permit movement in any direction of attack or defense. With the torso in *hanmi,* stand straight but with the feeling that the hips are ever so slightly lowered. Hold your head correctly, inclining neither up nor down, nor to right or left. The forward arm, slightly bent and protecting the side of the body should point between the opponent's nose and upper lip. The back arm should be bent and near the solar plexus. At this time, there should be no unnecessary power in such places as the elbows and the pit of the stomach. This becomes the posture of readiness, with the center of gravity in its natural position.

2. *Tachikata,* stance

Stand lightly, with your feet drawn slightly inward and a little bit closer together than in the front stance or rooted stance. Let the knees bend a little, and let the legs support the body weight equally. Power should be in the soles and toes, but the heels should feel as distant from the floor as the thickness of a sheet of paper. Stand lightly, keeping your composure.

3. *Me no tsukekata,* fixing the eyes

If you fasten your eyes on the opponent's face, you will lose sight of other things. When you are watching for his kick, you will not see his upper body. You must see all, from the top of his head to his toes. To take the measure of the opponent in front of you clearly, let your eyes feel as though they were looking at a distance object.

4. *Maai,* distance

When face to face with an opponent, the point of greatest importance in fighting strategy is distance. From a practical point of view, *maai* is the distance from which one can advance one step and deliver a decisive punch or kick; reciprocally, it is the distance from which can withdraw one step and protect himself from attack.

Maai differs to a greater or lesser extent according to individual physique and technique, but ideally it means to have the opponent away from you and to be close to him. Distancing has an important meaning in deciding victory or defeat, so it is very important to study and master advantageous *maai.*

5. *Waza o hodokoso kōki,* the psychological moment to execute a technique

Whether attacking by seizing the initiative earlier [*sen

no sen] or seizing the initiative later (*go no sen*), execution of a technique will have no effect unless advantage is taken of an opening. These are of three kinds: a mental opening, an opening in *kamae* and an opening in movements. The following pertains to the latter.

A. At the start of the opponent's technique. When the opponent, seeing an opening, begins his movement, at the very onset attack directly and instantly. His mind will be on his attack, and his defense insufficient. In that brief time, there can easily be an opening.

B. When the attack comes. When you are attacked, or or when there is a continuous attack that you block, and the opponent's strategic aims are exhausted and his techniques stop, attack.

C. When the mind is motionless. In the martial arts, there are strict warnings about being taken by surprise, being doubtful or vacillating. At the time a kick or punch is imminent, if one is seized by doubt or flinches in the face of the opponent's spirit, he will vacillate about launching his own attack, the body will stiffen, and a mental opening will occur. In this instant, there is a good possibility for a sudden, successful attack.

D. Creating an opening. When there is no opening on either side, a feint may be employed to distract the opponent. For example, a diversionary movement of the foot can draw his attention downward, making an attack to his upper body possible. There are many ways of doing this with the hand or foot, but if it is done clumsily, the opponent can find an opening. In practice, you must have good control of your own power and punch or kick with dead seriousness. One way is to execute continuous techniques that leave the opponent no room for counterattack. Then when his posture crumbles creating an opening, launch an instantaneous and decisive attack.

The above points should be studied carefully while practicing jiyū kumite. Although I repeat myself, I say again that in jiyū kumite, techniques are apt to end up in disarray. Therefore, training must be coordinated with kata, ippon jiyū kumite, etc., and great care must be taken to really learn fundamentals and to master strong techniques before all else.

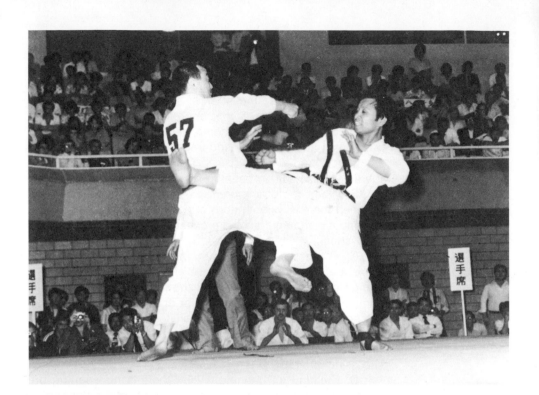

Second International Amateur Karate Federation Tournament, Tokyo, 1977

PREPARING FOR COMBAT

Understanding Training

From those who mastered the spirit of budō (martial arts), certain secret principles have been handed down from generation to generation. I introduce here a selection from these writings, which serve as a guide for training in kumite. Their practical application in deciding the issue of victory or defeat is not their only purpose; through them, one should come in contact with the spirit of the martial arts and judge himself. It remains then to practice karate-dō often and hard.

The stage of the novice

From the stage of being a novice, one gradually accumulates experience and reaches a superior level. He then returns to the stage of the novice.

This is true in the art of war. The novice knows neither how to hold the sword nor how to take a stance. His mind does not stop in his body. If he is attacked, he replies, but he has no strategy. Then, as the body learns techniques and postures, their uses and the strategems of battle, the mind is captivated by various things. When he tries to strike, he vacillates and becomes restricted. However, as months and years of training pile up, techniques and posture come to be applied without conscious effort. This is the stage of the novice. With detachment, with freedom from obstacles, appropriate movement becomes possible.

Takuan Zenji, *Fudō chishin myōroku*

The sword and Zen are one

Martial arts and Zen are in agreement on many points. Especially they dislike and forbid being attached to things. Both place great importance on this point. No matter how one may use techniques mastered in secret, if his mind becomes attached to techniques he cannot win. It is of the greatest importance in training that the mind does not become fixed, either on the enemy's movements or one's own movements, either on striking or blocking.

Yagyū Munenori, *Heihoka densho*

Striking truly

Striking truly is different from scoring a hit. In any way of striking, one must first determine how it is going to be, then do this authentically. Scoring a hit is only that, even if there is enough strength in it to kill the enemy. To strike truly means to decide in one's mind and to carry out the resolution of intent fully.

Miyamoto Musashi, *Gorin no sho*

This is very important in karate-dō and is connected with *kime-waza*, decisive technique. Musashi never took the easy attitude that winning was itself the significant thing. One of the points he taught was that if one cannot decide from the results whether victory was due to one's own strength or merely accidental, he will never reach a high level of skill.

Ken *and* tai

At the point of combat, launching the attack with singleminded concentration and seizing the initiative is *ken*. Not attacking suddenly, waiting for the enemy's charge, is *tai*.

From the viewpoint of mind and body, it is good to keep the mind in a state of reserve (*tai*) and the body in an active condition (*ken*). If the mind is too active, it is apt to run wild, leading to self-destruction. Vital to success is winning by letting the enemy make the first move. With this in mind, it is also said that even with the mind in *ken* and the body in *tai* advantage can be taken of the enemy's first move. The mind, though moving incessantly, is not unprepared, and the body, though in reserve, is ready to move. These two expressions are poles apart, but the meaning is the same: in either case to entice the enemy to act.

Yagyū Munenori, *Heihoka densho*

Outwardly calm, inwardly and outwardly active: listening to the sound of wind and water

Ken and *tai* are both inside and outside, leaning to neither. Inside, the *ki* [intrinsic energy] is working, moving, always attentive; outside is calm: this matches the laws of nature. Again, during a strong attack, if the mind is not drawn into the body's movements and remains calm, movement will not become confused. If the mind moves too, confusion occurs as a matter of course. *Ken-tai, dō-sei* are alternately inside and outside.

A bird on the surface of the water shows a placid exterior, but its webbed feet are active. In the same way, through accumulation of training, mind and body are brought together to be one thing. Then one acts with perfect freeness and can attain the highest level of martial training.

Yagyū Munenori, *Heihoka densho*

Sen

Two ways of taking the initiative

For seizing the initiative, there are *tai no sen* and *yu no sen*. Attacking head on from a fighting posture is *tai no sen*. Changing postures and attacking by taking advantage of circumstances is *yu no sen*.

In *tai no sen*, no motion is shown, frontal attack is made from *kamai*, and defenses are made as the situation demands. This means penetrating the enemy, breaking his defenses and attacking. In this case, tactics are primary, techniques secondary.

In *yu no sen*, attack comes from movements changing endlessly, defense from an unchanging posture. This means breaking the enemy's posture, outmaneuvering him and attacking. In this case, techniques are primary, tactics secondary.

Not knowing these things and attempting to win by attacking recklessly results in defeat. Understanding the uses of frontal attack and surprise attack can be the turning point between victory and defeat.

Kotōda Yahei, *Ittōsai sensei kempō sho*

In one breath

When the distance for striking is best, strike swiftly, in one breath, without making any preliminary movement. This is called *ichibyōshi*. The enemy may be on the verge of striking or escaping; while he wavers, finish the strike. Practice this well; learn to control it before the occasion arises. This must be mastered in training.

Miyamoto Musashi, *Gorin no sho*

In two beats

When the moment for striking is at hand, the enemy may suddenly withdraw or try to evade. At that time give the impression of striking. The enemy will experience momentary tenseness and a letdown. Strike then, without delay. In other words, make him relax. This is called *ni no koshi no hyōshi*.

Miyamoto Musashi, *Gorin no sho*

Three initiatives

There are three ways of taking the initiative.

One is to take the initiative with one's own attack—*ken no sen*.

Another is to take the initiative when the enemy attacks—*tai no sen*

A third is to take the initiative in both cases—*taitai no sen*.

In the beginning of any contest there are only these three

ways. According to the way the initiative is taken, victory can be obtained promptly.

Yagyū Shinkage-ryū

Go no Sen

Ways of blocking

When the enemy's territory has been entered and it is necessary to block his long sword, one's own short sword can be aimed at his eyes and and his long sword can be disposed of to one's right side. Again, his right eye can be aimed at and his long sword blocked by a thrust-block, as if clipping his neck. Another way is to think not of using the short sword to block but of aiming at his face with the left hand.

There are three ways, but in any of them, it is good to clench the right hand and aim for the enemy's face.

Miyamoto Musashi, Gorin no sho

The enemy's initiative

Win when the enemy strikes out.

If he charges without striking, win when he does strike.

Feint to induce an attack; win when he strikes.

In *ken no sen*, one way is to keep the body motionless and attack unexpectedly. Another way is while attacking strongly and quickly to keep the mind in reserve. Another is to tense the mind, approach the enemy briskly and coolly, and attack with great concentration. Another is to keep the mind unattached from beginning to end but attack strongly as with an enthusiasm coming from the bottom of the heart.

In *tai no sen*, when the enemy attacks, one way is to give the appearance of weakness without taking a posture. When he is close, jump back, then attack the point where he shows relaxation. Another way is when the enemy attacks to come forward with one strong step to upset his attacking rhythm; take advantage of this and victory can be won.

In *taitai no sen*, one way is to meet the enemy's sudden attack calmly but strongly. When he is close, attack his relaxed point from a strong posture in one breath. Another way is when the enemy attacks quietly to keep one's own body as if floating. When he is close, take a close look at his condition, then attack strongly.

Miyamoto Musashi, Gorin no sho

Second International Amateur Karate Federation Tournament, Tokyo, 1977

2
SEN NO SEN

SEN NO SEN

Seen from straight ahead, the initiation of Takeshi Ōishi's attack is something to behold. His *kamae* seems artlessly simple, but the thrust comes with fleeting swiftness, literally before there is time to say "Ah." His posture after the charge, in which he keeps his poise and complete control of his faculties (*zanshin*), is also beyond description. Thus, he is highly respected by karate enthusiasts around the world, and his uniqueness leaves others following in his wake.

In contrast to the half-baked practice of many, Ōishi follows up practice with more practice. Before taking up karate, he was one of the most highly skilled high school kendōka in Japan, and it was through kendō that he exhaustively learned leg *sabaki*, which is necessary also in karate. This took many years.

His timing is exemplary. Timing is so critical that to be off by as little as one-thousandth of a second can reverse the situation and make one the victim rather than the victor. Ōishi sees his opponent's movements second by second, knows his target, and attacks decisively. The technique he has of covering with his other hand at the same time is splendid, nearly flawless. Recently, he has often taken the initiative with a front kick.

Timing is important; so is rhythm, without which the initiative cannot be taken. In that fraction of time when whether to execute a technique or not is still undecided, it is best to dislocate *maai*. But at soon as it is readjusted, the technique should be executed without hesitation or vacillation.

In the pictures on the following pages, Ōishi's opponent is Shunsuke Takahashi, who also has an acknowledged reputation for the excellence of his techniques.

1

2

4

5

8

9

3

6

7

10

Punch vs. punch   When there is a chance, punch straight from the front without giving the opponent any leeway. Acting decisively is most important.

Timing of charge Charge in before the opponent's kick is completed. Posture and mental attitude after attack: be prepared to attack again.

1

2

3

Fumikomi Deflecting a kick to the left, stepping in with
fumikomi and a reverse punch requires swift leg movement.

33

Charging against upper level punch Jump close in and finish off (*kime*) with a lunge punch. The advancing leg must move rapidly, and the feeling should be that your hips will collide with the opponent's hips.

Charging against kick When the opponent bends his knee to kick, take the opportunity to spring deep inside, aiming for his chest. Cover your attack by using your other hand against the inside of his knee. Do not run away from the attacking leg (or arm). After the attack, again penetrate deeply.

Attack against kamae Charge straight in while the opponent is taking a stance, giving no thought to his block or counter-attack. Use the thrust of the pivot leg (*jiku ashi*) for a forceful attack.

Covering with the hand Punches or kicks, instead of being blocked, can be taken care of by using the hand as cover.

Practicing tsukkomi Most important is that the hand moves from its position of readiness directly to the target with absolutely no unnecessary motion. Timing must be perfect. This requires relaxed elbow, shoulders and knees.

3
GO NO SEN

GO NO SEN

A karateka who is expert in *go no sen* is Norihiko Iida. No matter who his opponent is, he keeps his own pace.

Go no sen, taking the initiative later, is not the same thing as counterattacking or engaging in defensive karate, nor is it simply inducing the opponent to action. It means to lead the opponent into movements advantageous to one's own self and then finishing off according to one's own pace.

Iida's changing techniques are admirable. They bring to mind the mysterious technique of twirling one's fingers as if to hypnotize a dragonfly. One never thinks he will fall for this trick, but in the end he succumbs. A case in point occurred in a recent international tournament when Iida performed a grand technique, going from a roundhouse kick to a double kick, which left the spectators speechless.

Essential to *go no sen* is *kihaku*, which is spirit. By overwhelming the opponent with your spirit, you can induce him to action and defeat him. In a word, spirit is the cardinal point in victory. Thus training the sixth sense is crucial for distancing, as mentioned earlier. In *maai*, one must see *all*.

To have the ability to let a punch or kick come very close and still have the confidence to block and counterattack requires daily practice. And it must be understood fully that a block is not simply that; it must be followed in a flash by the destruction of the opponent's fighting posture. The effectiveness is then much greater.

Taking a *kamae* in the front stance, shift to a back stance without moving the feet. Dodge the opponent's fist or kick by moving the torso backward. Then let the thrust from the back leg move the torso forward and counterattack.

In the pictures on the following pages, Iida's opponent is Yoshiharu Ōsaka, a karateka whose basic techniques are penetrating and whose kata are of the first rank.

1

2

4

5

7

8

3

6

9

Ashi barai When the opponent charges, throw him over your leg, finish with a punch.

1

2

Ashi barai While using your leg to destroy the opponent's stability, finish him off.

Gedan barai uke Blocking the kick downward, turn the opponent around. Execute a finishing blow without giving him room to recover his stance.

5

6

Sukui-uke Bending backward, draw opponent close and block. Use spring of hips to regain stance, counterattack.

1

3

4

2

Iida's kamae is worth studying carefully. Leading his opponent to attack, feinting an opening, threatening, he captures the initiative. He may, for example, seem ready to take a thrust kick, then block it.

Go no sen is not a defensive posture; your stance must overflow with fighting spirit. Never surrender the initiative.

1

2

Reliable blocking In *go no sen,* reliable, effective blocking against any attack is very important. Block to the outside, away from your own body.

Destroying the opponent When blocking, also destroy the opponent's balance and stability, thus setting the stage for *kime*. Use your advancing leg against his advancing leg, pushing his knee outward from the inside or inward from the outside.

Training in ducking To bring the opponent as close as possible, you must understand his attacking movements completely. Temper this skill by changing from front stance to back stance and bending the torso backward to avoid the attack. Against punch or kick, you can block easily, then counterattack strongly using the spring of the torso when returning to the front stance.

54

Second International Amateur Karate Federation Tournament, Tokyo 1977

4
TYPES OF KICKS

TYPES OF KICKS

The hands and feet of Masaaki Ueki are worth watching, for they are very fast and truly sharp. His kick can be heard from some distance away, and he exhibits sharpness and great power in bending his knee. It is not surprising that many opponents have been defeated.

Thinking of the ideal kick, his balance, supporting ankle, dynamic use of the knee and execution are nearly faultless. In tournaments, his spirit and timing are very impressive. He may arrest an opponent's movement momentarily by pressing the other's advancing leg with his own sword foot or sole and immediately change techniques and kick. He can also make effective use of *keri-nuke,* which is to slip through the enemy by kicking. Recently, those who have mastered this are few.

Succeeding in *sen no sen* by kicking is difficult. The motion at the very beginning of the kick is visible, the opponent's counterattack rather easy. That is why the bending of the knee must be exceedingly fast. Thus, balance from the supporting leg, which can be nothing less than perfect, is the indispensable condition. The motto to be kept in mind in daily training is: small motion, large kick, sharp and powerful.

In the pictures on the following pages, Ueki's opponent is Mikio Yahara. His quick-witted changing techniques (*henka waza*) very frequently catch the opponent by surprise, and he has a reputation for *shobu-zuyosa* (snatching victory from the jaws of defeat).

3

6

9

1

2

3

Kekomi When the opponent is about to attack, aim a strong thrust kick at his solar plexus or throat.

1

2

1

2

4

5

Keri-nuke After a sharp front kick to the solar plexus, get behind the opponent by sliding the supporting foot. In this kick, it is important to lower the hips while moving the supporting leg.

64

3

6

7

Shifting body weight and hips From a wide stance, bring the front foot back lightly at the beginning of the opponent's attack. As soon as body weight is shifted, counterattack to shoulder or face with thrust kick.

Bending the knee and thrusting the hips forward Make the front leg the supporting leg, bending the ankle and knee and carrying all the body weight on it. When raising the knee of the kicking leg to the chest—quickly, lightly and smoothly—bend the other ankle more and thrust the hips forward sharply for a strong kick.

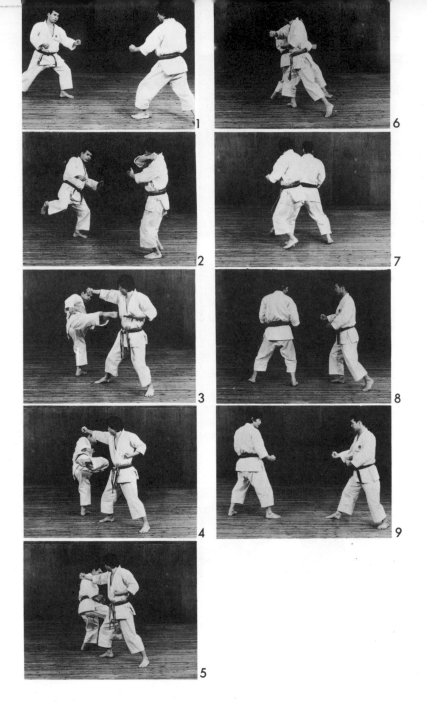

Keri-nuke At the time the opponent attacks, while lowering the hips and sliding the supporting leg close to him deliver a small-scale but sharp front kick or roundhouse kick and move to his rear. Stable body movement is important as is returning the kicking foot to the floor rapidly and shifting the body weight to

it immediately. As important as the kick itself is the sliding of the supporting leg, the ankle and knee of which are bent but strong and flexible. The *keri-nuke* is very effective but also very difficult. Practice diligently with the important points always in mind.

Second International Amateur Karate Federation Tournament, Tokyo, 1977

5
STRIKING

STRIKING IN CLOSE COMBAT

Keigo Abe's forte are back-fist and other striking techniques. He has a great number of small scale techniques, and these are extremely varied, as many a losing opponent has discovered.

Against an intense attack, he will move to the side and retaliate with a back-fist or sword hand. Turning the hips with the pivot leg as the core of the movement, the arm, leg and hip movements are precisely coordinated for a splendidly effective technique.

In striking, *maai* and handling the body (*tai-sabaki*) are intimately related. One reason for Abe's excellence is the way he can lead the opponent's attack, move out of the way and counterattack an instant before the end of the opponent's technique. There are various ways to induce an attack: narrowing the distance, overwhelming the opponent with one's fighting spirit, withdrawing, making the opponent think there is an opening and so on. Either front or back leg may be the pivot leg; move in close to the opponent's body and use the power of hip rotation. When any technique is executed, spiritual energy must be at its fullest.

In the pictures on the following pages, Abe's opponent is Mikio Yahara.

1

2

4

5

7

74

3

6

8

1

2

Back-fist strike After leading the opponent to attack first make your front leg the pivot leg and with a sharp rotation of the hips, counterattack to the face with the back-fist.

3

4

5

1

2

3

4

Sword hand strike   Against a kick, advance a step and finish off
with a sword hand strike, outside inward.

1

2

3

4

Sword hand strike   While scoop-blocking a front kick with left hand, attack carotid artery with right sword hand.

1

2

3

Tai sabaki   Turning on the pivot leg, use the reverse rotation of the hips in a back-fist strike. Coordinating breathing, rotation and arm and foot movements requires training.

4

5

1

2

3

4

Throwing opponent While rotating hips to left, use left hand for scooping block and right hand for sword hand strike to neck. Then, rotating hips widely to right, have the feeling of withdrawing left hand and pushing down right hand.

Ridge hand strike Take care of the opponent's punch by sweeping it to the side with the left hand. Then, in unison with the rotation of the hips, counterattack to the carotid artery with a wide ridge hand strike from the outside.

1

2

3

Some close combat techniques
1. Upward elbow strike while checking opponent's punch.
2. Upward elbow strike while checking opponent's kick.
3. Side elbow strike after checking opponent's punching arm.
4. *Tai-sabaki*, sinking hips, and horizontal back-fist strike.
5. Chicken-head wrist strike to jaw after checking kick.
6. Elbow (or back-fist) strike while checking opponent's hand with your hand, or his foot with your foot.
7. Knee to solar plexus after blocking strike with both hands.
8. At onset of opponent's kick, charge in close, upset his balance, then ridge hand strike to neck.

84

4

5

6

7

8

Second International Amateur Karate Federation Tournament, Tokyo, 1977

6
KICKING

KICKING IN CLOSE COMBAT

In close combat, Katsunori Tsuyama's roundhouse kick has very often come as a complete surprise. Delivered from the front, the target may be the back of the head. He is especially adept at catching the opponent's punching arm and, while pulling him closer, executing a sharp roundhouse kick aimed at the jaw from very close range. Using a higher arc, he can aim a kick at the back of the opponent's neck with the toes slanting downward. This unique ability is inconceivable without hips of extraordinary strength and flexibility. Tsuyama has such hips only because of the accumulated effect of honest training in fundamentals over a long period of years.

The roundhouse kick is often used in contests nowadays, but one in which the leg travels a high course toward the objective and the ankle is twisted and the toes point diagonally downward—a solid technique of actual combat—is seldom seen. It is regrettable that the number of karateka who train strictly and with perseverance to master fundamental techniques has become fewer. Tsuyama's balance and the course his kicking leg travels thus stand out all the more brilliantly.

The supporting foot is first slid close to the opponent's foot, the ankle bent and the sole solidly on the floor, so that one has a firm stand for executing the kick. The path to improvement is repeated practice in raising the knee of the kicking leg to chest level.

In the pictures on the following pages, Tsuyama's opponent is Eishige Matsukura, who through an abundance of extensive training has developed strong legs and hips that give him command of powerful strikes and kicks.

1

2

4

5

7

8

3

6

Roundhouse kick after kicking attack   As soon as opponent's kicking foot touches the floor, counterattack to face with a high roundhouse kick. This is very difficult unless the knee comes very high and very close to the chest.
The points are the same for a kick from inside outward.

1

2

1
2

5
6

Balance and course of kicking leg   When the opponent begins to attack, slide deep in towards his rear. Penetrate his dead space and deliver a surprise attack, a roundhouse kick to the cervical vertebrae. Balance and correct route are essential. Roundhouse kick. A strong, effective kick can be executed by raising the leg high, twisting the ankle and attacking diagonally downward.

4

7

Kicking while pulling opponent in Against an upper level attack, catch the opponent's punching arm and pull him toward you, then kick his side with your rear foot.

Bending the knee Raise the knee very high (to shoulder level) and swing the leg from the outside. The kick will be more effective if the toes point downward. With practice, the kick can be executed without swinging the leg far from the body. This is a cross between a front kick and a roundhouse kick.

7
THROWING

ROTATION, TAI-SABAKI, THROWING

Tetsuhiko Asai's ever-changing movements, sometimes resembling a dance performed in the air, leave spectators gaping with admiration. Dodging under a kicking leg, striking to the groin from below, escaping an attack by a paper thin margin, leaping for a sword hand attack to the opponent's neck, landing and reversing direction for a leg sweep—such intricate and acrobatic feats as these, which are of actual use in combat, he performs in kumite. He probably has no equals.

His inimitable talent has its source in training since youth, fostering powerful hips, a flexible body, deep technical skill, excellent reflexes and nerveless courage.

For continuous movement, *tai-sabaki* and the ability to change direction are necessary, and for these sharp use of the hips and agile leg movements are indispensable. In rotating the hips, there are several possibilities: to right or left toward the front; to right or left toward the back; when turning, either the right or left hip may be the fulcrum, or the center of the hips may be the axis for a comma-shaped movement. In leg movements, there are moving forward or backward, left or right, by crossing one leg in front of or behind the other (left to right, or right to left); moving forward or backward, or left or right, by changing the pivot leg, without crossing the legs; moving forward or backward, left or right, by keeping the same distance between the feet and using *yori-ashi*.

In the pictures on the following pages, Asai's opponent is Yoshiharu Ōsaka.

1

2

5

6

3   4

7

Jumping and throwing When the opponent charges, put your hand on his shoulder and jump to his rear. Finish with sword hand and pull him down.

Jumping and sword hand With front leg as pivot leg, go to opponent's rear. Follow elbow strike with sword hand strike.

Rotation, reverse rotation, ashi barai Blocking attack from the right, rotate for back roundhouse kick. Then, using reverse rotation, execute *ashi barai* and back-fist for *kime*.

106

6

7

8

9

Ducking a kick After ducking, counterattack while moving to opponent's rear. Surprise value is great.

3

6

7

Throwing Against successive kicks and punches, grab opponent's wrist, turn, lower hips and throw him.

3

4

8

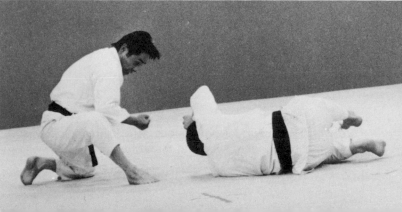

9

1

2

3

Throwing When under continuous attack, lower body suddenly, scoop opponent's leg and throw him.

4

5

6

Penetrating tai-sabaki and pulling down In timing with opponent's attack, slide in close to his body. Stay close and get behind him, by using sharp hip rotation, then pull him down.

114

3

4

8

9

Jumping sword hand strike   Jumping close to the opponent's fist, execute a sword hand strike from above while going to his rear. When jumping, bring both knees to chest level to make strike more effective.

Sliding foot, moving foot   There is the tactic of sliding the left foot in close to the opponent's back foot and getting close to his back. Arai does this elusively by having mastered basic sliding and moving foot techniques.

1

2

3

Ducking   Decisiveness is the most important point in ducking a kick. After turning the head with good timing, direct it toward the opponent's groin. Go instantly to the counterattack by making a reverse turn.

118

4

5

6

1

2

3

4

1

2

3

Ducking The preparatory practice to ducking a kick is learning to duck a punch. First block, then duck towards opponent's armpit. When this is learned, duck without blocking. Swinging the torso is necessary in this case.

Back roundhouse kick, reverse rotation After blocking by rotating on the front pivot leg, carry out reverse rotation and sweep opponent's leg with kicking leg. Balance must be extremely good, and legs and loins very flexible.

6

8

7

9

10

123

Essentials of back roundhouse kick Make advancing right foot the pivot foot, and immediately after blocking with both hands, rotate hips widely to the left. If ankle and knee are not bent and stable, kick will not be effective.

Reverse rotation, ashi barai With right leg as pivot leg, rotate hips widely to the left and sweep opponent's ankle or knee with left kicking leg. This will be effective only if supporting leg, hips and kicking leg turn simultaneously.

Second International Amateur Karate Federation Tournament, Tokyo, 1977

8
TWO-LEVEL ATTACK

TWO-LEVEL ATTACK

With a variety of reciprocal and continuous techniques, but without any superfluous movements, Hirokazu Kanazawa engages and brings down the opponent. Attacking, he searches out the opponent's reply, then changes to another technique for the finish. His tactics in all directions are excellence, and as seen from his record, he applies *kime-waza*—punching, striking and kicking—quite appropriately.

Movements are not simply that; finely coordinated with them are techniques on a large scale, freely executed. From movement (*dō*) to inactivity (*sei*), use of chance, timing—all are done remarkably well. When under attack, Kanazawa executes *tai-sabaki* a split second faster than the opponent's movement.

In avoiding an attack by shifting the body or lowering the hips, one can leave oneself open to continuous attack and be driven into a corner. Thus, after avoiding the attack, one must change direction and immediately counterattack while moving. When the opponent charges, it is more effective not to oppose the force directly; rather cope with it by a block deflecting the strike or kick to the side of one's own body. While doing this, the opponent's balance can be upset with the counterattack. In shifting from handling an attack to attacking, there is the possibility of giving great force to the techniques by breathing, concentration of the spirit and the instantaneous maximal tensing of the muscles. This must occur at the same time the center of gravity is shifted.

In the pictures on the following pages, Kanazawa's opponent is Yoshiharu Ōsaka.

1

2

5

6

3

4

7

1

2

5

6

3

4

7

8

1

2

3

Kicking, mawarikomi, ridge hand strike   Execute a front kick to lead the opponent into a kicking counterattack. At the same time you block, finish off with a ridge hand strike to the carotid artery.

4

5

6

7

1

2

3

4

Lunge punch and variations   First lead opponent into blocking.
Then block his counterattack and finish off.

Exhibition match between Kanazawa and Asai. 2. Individual
kamae. 3. Asai's sudden roundhouse kick. 4. Kanazawa's
sword hand attack to face. 5–6. Asai dodges Kanazawa's
kick. 7. Small-scale techniques. 8. Kanazawa's thrust kick.
9. Match restarts. 10–11. Asai's thrust kick. 12–13. Repeated
exchanges. 14–16. Asai avoids attack by ducking. 17. Glaring,
both men withdraw.

3

4

5

6

7

8

9

10

11

12

13

14

15

16

17

18

GLOSSARY